Fact Finders®

EXCEPTIONAL ENGI

EXTRAORDINARY
BRIDGES

by Sonya Newland

CAPSTONE PRESS
a capstone imprint

Fact Finders Books are published by Capstone Press,
1710 Roe Crest Drive, North Mankato, Minnesota 56003
www.mycapstone.com

Produced for Capstone Publishers by
White-Thomson Publishing Ltd
www.wtpub.co.uk

Library of Congress Cataloging-in-Publication Data
Names: Newland, Sonya, author.
Title: Extraordinary Bridges: The Science of How and Why They Were Built/by Sonya Newland.
Description: North Mankato, Minnesota: Capstone Press, [2019] | Series: Fact Finders.
   Exceptional Engineering | Includes bibliographical references and index. | Audience: Ages 8–10.
Identifiers: LCCN 2018010609 (print) | LCCN 2018013668 (ebook) | ISBN 9781543529074 (library binding) |
   ISBN 9781543529128 (paperback) | ISBN 9781543529166 (eBook PDF)
Subjects: LCSH: Bridges—Design and Construction—Juvenile literature. | Historic bridges—Juvenile literature.
Classification: LCC TG148 (ebook) | LCC TG148.N49 2019 (print) | DDC 624.209—dc23
LC record available at https://lccn.loc.gov/2018010609

Editorial Credits
Editor: Sonya Newland
Designer: Steve Mead
Media Researcher: Sonya Newland
Production Specialist: Laura Manthe

Photo Credits
Alamy: IanDagnall Computing, 19, David R. Frazier Photolibrary, Inc., 25; Getty Images: The Sydney Morning Herald,
15, 16, Fairfax Media, 17, Underwood Archives, 20, 21; iStock: LianeM, 4, Wavetop, 6t, DieterMeyrl, 6b, Peter–Horvath,
8–9, narawon, 10, jsteck, 11, chapin31, 13b, qizai00, 18, 35007, 28, efired, 29; Julian Baker: 5, 13t, 23, 27; Shutterstock:
somchaij, cover, Pamela Uyttendaele, 7, Taki O, 14, pisaphotography, 22, shannon white-diecidue, 24, ra66, 26.

Design elements by Shutterstock

TABLE OF CONTENTS

CHAPTER 1

PONT DU GARD

People have been building bridges since prehistoric times. Early bridges were simple wooden beams laid across water. As tools and technology developed, bigger and stronger bridges were constructed to cross much larger areas of water or land. You might recognize some of the world's most famous bridges, but how much do you know about their engineering and the stories behind why they were built?

The Pont du Gard is made of **limestone** blocks taken from a nearby **quarry**. The blocks were carried on boats down the river to the bridge site.

limestone—a hard rock formed from the remains of ancient sea creatures

quarry—a place where stone or other minerals are dug from the ground

The Pont du Gard is an amazing example of ancient engineering. It was built by the Romans in around AD 50. Stretching across the River Gardon in France, this arch bridge is 902 feet (275 meters) long and 155 feet (47 m) high.

In the 1st century AD, France was part of the Roman Empire. At the time, there was not enough water in the city of Nîmes for all the people who lived there. So the Romans decided to build an **aqueduct**. This would transport water from a **spring** in Uzès, 31 miles (50 kilometers) away from Nîmes. The Romans built pipes under the ground to guide the water. But halfway to Nîmes, they ran into the River Gardon flowing through a **gorge**. To get the water across the river, they needed a bridge.

TYPES OF BRIDGES

A *beam bridge* is a single beam supported by **piers** or columns.

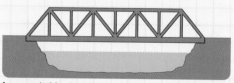

A *truss bridge* is a beam bridge strengthened with triangular frames.

An *arch bridge* is a curved arch, with **abutments** at each end.

In a *suspension bridge*, the road "hangs" from cables secured by huge blocks at each end.

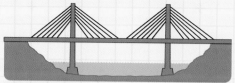

In a *cable-stayed bridge*, the road is supported by cables connected to a tower.

aqueduct—an artificial channel for carrying water, typically a large bridge across a river or valley

spring—a place where water rises to the surface from an underground source

gorge—a canyon with steep walls that rise straight upward

pier—an upright structure that supports a bridge or arch

abutment—a concrete support at the end of a bridge

The stones used to make the arches were cut carefully so they fit together perfectly. There was no need for cement to hold them together.

The Pont du Gard has three levels. Each level has a different number of arches. There are six on the lower level, the largest of which is 80 feet (24 m) wide. On the middle level are 11 arches. The widest arch there is also 80 feet (24 m). There were 38 arches on the top level, but only 35 remain today. They are all 15 feet (4.6 m) wide.

The upper level joined the land on each side of the river above the gorge. A **channel** of carved stone was added along the top of the aqueduct. This carried the water from the spring across the river.

THE ROMAN ARCH

Small arches had been used for 2,000 years before the Romans. But the Romans found a way to build much larger arches. They used concrete, which is a mixture of sand and **lime**. Using concrete made Roman arches incredibly strong. After the concrete hardened, it was cut into wedge-shaped blocks that fit together in a semicircle. The top center stone—the keystone—was the last to be added.

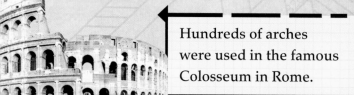

Hundreds of arches were used in the famous Colosseum in Rome.

channel—a path that directs water through or across something

lime—a white substance that is made by burning limestone and used to make cement

The Romans planned and built the Pont du Gard very carefully. We know this because some of the stones have numbers carved into them. The numbers told the builders in which order to use the blocks. Marks on other stones suggest they may have supported **scaffolding**.

The Pont du Gard probably took about five years to complete. **Historians** believe that between 800 and 1,000 men may have worked on it in that time.

Did You Know?

It takes around 24 hours for water to travel from its source in Uzès to Nîmes.

The aqueduct ended in a tank in Nîmes. From there, pipes carried the water all over the city.

scaffolding—a temporary framework or set of platforms used to support workers and materials

historian—a person who studies events that happened in the past

CHAPTER 2

PONTE VECCHIO

The Ponte Vecchio is a famous bridge in Florence, Italy. The lower level of the bridge was completed in 1345. It was designed using segmental arches. These are wider and flatter than the semicircular Roman arches. Three arches were used in the Ponte Vecchio.

The bridge was designed to help defend the city against attack. It had four strong guard towers—two at each end. These were joined by strong walls with **battlements** along both sides.

battlement—a low wall (as at the top of a castle or a tower) with open spaces to shoot through

In 1565 the Duke of Florence added another level to the bridge. The duke had palaces on both sides of the river. He wanted to move between them easily and privately. Architect Giorgio Vasari designed the upper walkway for the duke. Today it is known as the "Vasari corridor."

Did You Know?

Lining the bridge were 43 shops. But in the mid-1300s, buildings were not allowed to block public walkways. This meant that the shopkeepers could not extend their shops toward the inside of the bridge, where people walked. To get around this law, the shopkeepers in the Ponte Vecchio extended their shops out over the river instead.

The Ponte Vecchio crosses the River Arno. The bridge is 105 feet (32 m) at its widest.

CHAPTER 3

ROYAL GORGE BRIDGE

When it opened in 1929, the Royal Gorge Bridge was the highest in the world. At 955 feet (291 m), it held that record for 72 years. It was beaten by the Liuguanghe Bridge in China in 2001.

The Royal Gorge Bridge crosses the gorge near Cañon City, Colorado. A man named Lon P. Piper came up with the idea for the bridge. He wanted people to be able to enjoy the stunning views over the gorge. Today the bridge attracts more than 300,000 visitors a year.

In total, the Royal Gorge Bridge is 1,260 feet (384 m) long, including the approaches.

SUSPENSION CABLES

The deck on a suspension bridge is supported by vertical cables. These hang from other cables, which run between towers at each end of the bridge. Early suspension bridges used rope for the cables. Later, chains were used. Today most suspension bridges have cables made from thousands of **steel** wires bound together, which are extremely strong.

Designers planned a suspension bridge to cross the gorge. The main **span** needed to be 880 feet (268 m) long. To achieve this, **engineer** George Cole used two cables. Each cable was made of 2,100 steel strands.

The cables were attached to two steel towers. In suspension bridges the towers support most of the weight, so they need to be very strong. The towers in the Royal Gorge were fixed in huge concrete pillars built lower down. The concrete for these bases was made from crushed **granite**, which had been dug out of the gorge.

The towers stand 150 feet (46 m) high.

Did You Know?

Steel is the perfect material for creating strong cables. A single steel wire less than 0.1 inch (0.25 centimeters) thick can support more than 1,000 pounds (454 kilograms).

steel—a hard, strong metal made from mostly iron and carbon

span—the length of a bridge from end to end

engineer—someone trained to design and build machines, vehicles, bridges, roads, or other structures

granite—a very hard rock used in construction

Finally the deck was laid. More than 1,200 planks of wood had to be bolted to the steel deck frame. This roadway was designed mainly for people to walk across, but it can also be used by cars. However, because the bridge does not have a **truss**, the deck shakes when vehicles cross. Two cables were later added beneath the bridge to reduce the shaking.

Suspension Bridges with the Longest Central Spans

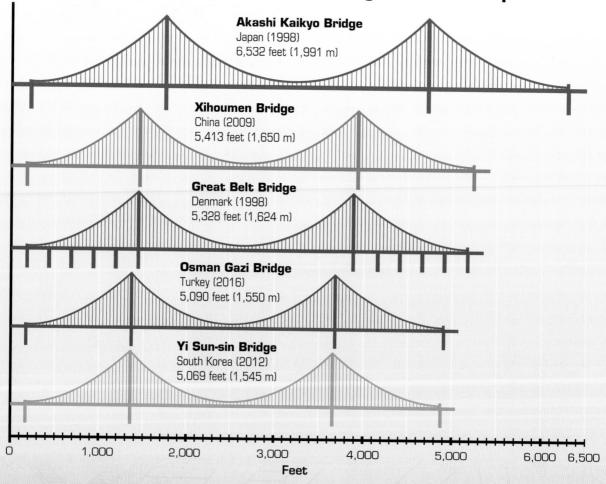

Akashi Kaikyo Bridge
Japan (1998)
6,532 feet (1,991 m)

Xihoumen Bridge
China (2009)
5,413 feet (1,650 m)

Great Belt Bridge
Denmark (1998)
5,328 feet (1,624 m)

Osman Gazi Bridge
Turkey (2016)
5,090 feet (1,550 m)

Yi Sun-sin Bridge
South Korea (2012)
5,069 feet (1,545 m)

Feet

truss—a framework of metal or wooden beams used to support objects, such as bridges, walls, or roofs

BUILD A SUSPENSION BRIDGE

To see how a suspension bridge works, try building your own. Use a strip of cardboard for the deck. Glue craft sticks together to make two towers in an H shape. Each end of the deck should rest on the bar of the H. Attach string to one corner of the deck, then run it up to the top of one tower and along to the other tower. Secure it at the far end of the deck. The string should be slightly loose so it dips in the middle. Do this on both sides to make the main cables. Attach more string from the main cables to the deck to make the suspension cables.

How much weight can your suspension bridge hold? If you make your bridge longer, what effect does this have?

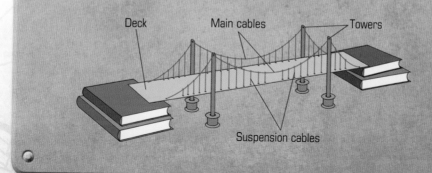

Deck   Main cables   Towers

Suspension cables

Steel barriers keep people on the bridge safe.

CHAPTER 4

SYDNEY HARBOUR BRIDGE

A bridge across Sydney Harbour in Australia was first suggested in 1815. However, it was more than 100 years before the idea really began to take shape.

In 1922 engineer John Bradfield designed a steel arch bridge. It would join Millers Point in Sydney with Milsons Point on the harbor's north shore. Two huge workshops were built at Milsons Point. Most of the bridge was constructed there.

The Sydney Harbour Bridge took nearly nine years to build.

Did You Know?

There are two towers at each end of Sydney Harbour Bridge. Each tower is 292 feet (89 m) high. They are made of concrete covered in granite. The granite came from a quarry 186 miles (300 km) south of Sydney. Three ships were built to transport the granite up the coast to the bridge site.

The bridge was designed with four main **bearings**. Bearings are the parts of a bridge that each end of the deck rests on. They allow the bridge to move slightly. This transfers some of the stress from the surface to the structure below ground. Bearings make a bridge strong and safe. To support the bearings, workers dug **foundations** 40 feet (12 m) deep. They filled the foundations with concrete made of cement, sand, and crushed granite.

Approach spans are roads leading onto a bridge. Work began on these in 1925.

bearing—the part of a bridge that the main deck or walkway rests on at each end
foundation—a base on which something rests or is built

Sydney Harbour is very deep. In fact, it is so deep that structures could not be set up to allow workers to build the arch from below. Instead, two large "creeper cranes" were constructed. These allowed workers to build the arch out from the land on each side of the harbor. As each piece of the bridge was being placed, it was secured by long cables that ran underground.

As work progressed and the bridge became larger, the steel sections were towed out into the harbor and lifted into place. In August 1930 crowds gathered to watch the two sides meet in the middle. Once the they were joined, the underground cables were removed.

Creeper cranes were heavy cranes with hoists and cradles to lift materials (and workers) into position.

Did You Know?

Heat makes steel expand—and there is a lot of steel in the Sydney Harbour Bridge! Huge hinges at the bottom of the four towers allow some movement, so the entire bridge can expand in the hot Sydney sun.

Next, the cranes worked back out toward the edges, hanging the steel decking as they went. Concrete roads and walkways were laid on the deck, and tracks were added for trains. Today the Sydney Harbour bridge has eight vehicle lanes, two train tracks, a pedestrian walkway, and a bicycle path.

The bridge opened in March 1932. At 3,770 feet (1,149 m) long, it was an amazing engineering achievement. The huge arch spans 1,650 feet (503 m) and reaches 440 feet (134 m) above sea level. About 58,200 tons (52,800 tonnes) of steel were used to build it. The steel plates are held together by 6 million steel **rivets**. Every single rivet was put in by hand.

The first piece of roadway is placed on the Sydney Harbour Bridge. It is suspended by steel cables.

CHAPTER 5

GOLDEN GATE BRIDGE

The Golden Gate **Strait** joins the Pacific Ocean and San Francisco Bay. In the early 20th century, people began talking about building a bridge across it. But everyone said that it was impossible or that it would be too expensive. Engineer Joseph Strauss believed it could be done.

More than 100,000 vehicles cross the Golden Gate Bridge every day.

Did You Know?

The Golden Gate Bridge is famous for its bright orange-red color. The color was chosen so that the bridge would stand out against the blue of the sea and sky. It also helps ships passing through the strait see the bridge in the fog that often covers the area.

strait—a narrow waterway connecting two large bodies of water

Work began on the supporting structures in 1933. Abutments were built on each side of the water. Later that year the north tower began taking shape. But when it came to the south tower, engineers faced a new challenge. Positioned out in the strait, the foundations for the second tower had to be laid underwater.

A long platform was built out from the shore to the place where the tower needed to be. Divers then dove more than 100 feet (30 m) underwater. There, they blasted away the rock from the seabed and laid the concrete foundations.

A long suspension bridge needs tall towers. The Golden Gate's towers are 746 feet (227 m) high. They were designed in a popular style of the 1930s called Art Deco.

Once the towers were complete, work could begin on the cables. These were hung using a method called "cable-spinning." Wires were wound around spools like thread. They were carried back and forth across the bridge on a system of spinning wheels. All the individual wires were then bound together to make cables. The company employed to construct the cables had been given a year to finish the job. They completed the task in six months.

Did You Know?

Each cable was 7,650 feet (2,332 m) long and was made of around 27,500 individual wires. That's about 80,000 miles (130,000 km) of wire!

A "catwalk" was constructed so men could work high up on the wires. Workers wore safety ropes in case they fell.

Next came the deck. Workers started at the towers and moved out over the water, putting the pieces in place as they went. Each section was hung from the suspension cables. To strengthen the deck, steel trusses were added all along it.

The Golden Gate Bridge opened in 1937. At 8,981 feet (2,737 m), it was the longest suspension bridge in the world at the time. It was also the tallest, thanks to its towers. Those records have since been beaten, but the Golden Gate remains one of the most famous bridges ever built.

No temporary supports were needed for the roadway because it was hung from the cables piece by piece.

Golden Gate Bridge Timeline

January 5, 1933
The first ground is broken and work begins.

June 28, 1935
The San Francisco tower is completed.

November 18, 1936
The two sections of the bridge span meet in the middle.

1933 **1934** **1935** **1936** **1937**

November 7, 1933
Work begins on the Marin tower.

October 1935
Main cable-spinning begins.

January 19, 1937
The first part of the roadway is laid.

May 28, 1937
The bridge opens to vehicles.

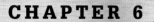

CHAPTER 6

LAKE PONTCHARTRAIN CAUSEWAY

Beam bridges are the simplest type of bridge. They have a main span and an abutment at each end. Because they have no support in the middle, single beam bridges cannot be very long. However, several beam bridges can be joined together to make a "continuous span." Some of the longest bridges in the world are beam bridges. The Lake Pontchartrain Causeway in Louisiana, is a good example. It is around 24 miles (38 km) long.

Did You Know?

For 8 miles (13 km) on the causeway, you cannot see land in any direction. This makes for a rather scary drive!

BUILD A BEAM BRIDGE

Simple beam bridges cannot bear much weight. Think about what happens when you walk across a beam of wood. It begins to bend as you get closer to the middle. Your weight makes the top surface compress (push downward) and the bottom stretch. Changing the shape of a beam bridge can make it stronger.

Try building your own beam bridge by first setting two piles of books 6 inches (15 cm) apart. These will act as bridge supports. Put a thin piece of cardboard on top of the supports. Place pennies on your cardboard "bridge," one by one. How many pennies can you place before it collapses?

Now fold up the long edges of the cardboard to make sides. Put it back on the supports and add pennies again. How many can you add this time before it collapses?

Try changing the height of the sides or folding the cardboard in different shapes. How do these changes affect the strength of the bridge?

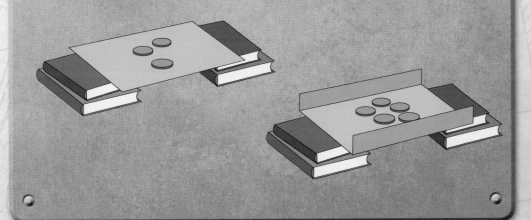

Lake Pontchartrain covers around 630 square miles (1,632 square kilometers). New Orleans lies on the shore of the lake. In the 1950s the population of the city began to increase. It was not long before people grew tired of driving all the way around the lake. They began to consider how to build a bridge across it so they could reach the other side more quickly. The project got the go-ahead in 1955.

Because the soil under the lake is very soft, engineers had to design very strong, very long **pilings**. These were hollow concrete tubes that were made to be extra strong. They were driven deep into the ground beneath the lake to make sure they were really sturdy.

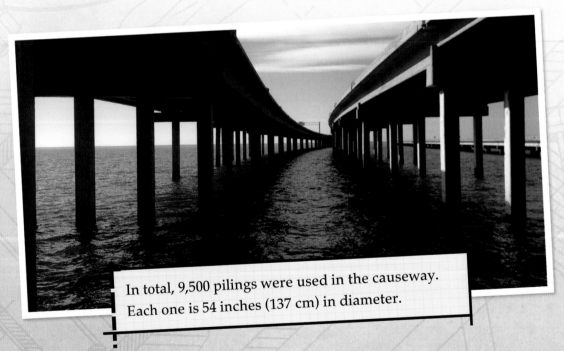

In total, 9,500 pilings were used in the causeway. Each one is 54 inches (137 cm) in diameter.

pilings—a heavy wood or steel pole or beam that is driven into the ground to support a bridge or pier

The concrete pilings and the deck were made in a factory built at one end of the bridge. The deck was then created in sections, which were fixed in place one at a time. As the bridge got longer, barges carried the sections out onto the lake.

The causeway is actually two separate bridges running **parallel** to each other. The first was completed in 1956. The second bridge opened in 1969. The two bridges are 80 feet (24 m) apart and are joined by seven crossovers. Not only do the crossovers connect the two bridges, they are also places where drivers can pull over in emergencies.

Both bridges have a bascule, which is a type of drawbridge. It can be raised to let tall boats on the lake pass underneath.

parallel—an equal distance apart at all points

assembly line—an arrangement where work passes from one person to the next person until the job is done

CHAPTER 7

LANGKAWI SKY BRIDGE

The Langkawi Sky Bridge, high up in the mountains of Malaysia, opened in 2005. Mahathir Mohamad, the prime minister at the time, came up with the idea. He wanted people to be able to admire the great natural beauty of this area.

The Langkawi Sky Bridge was built 3,000 feet (700 m) up in Mount Mat Cincang Geo Park.

Peter Wyss, the man who designed the Langkawi Sky Bridge, wanted it to be as simple and beautiful as the scenery around it. He did not want it to have lots of cables like a suspension bridge. Instead, he chose a cable-stayed structure. This meant that the bridge only needed eight cables, which are attached to a single steel tower. The tower was sunk into a huge concrete block built at the bottom of a gorge in the mountains. The tower is 270 feet (82 m) tall.

WHY CHOOSE A CABLE-STAYED BRIDGE?

Cable-stayed bridges are very stable. They are also cheaper to build than suspension bridges. In a cable-stayed bridge, strong steel cables support the deck. These cables connect the deck to the top of a single tower. To balance the weight of the bridge evenly, the tower is usually located in the middle of the bridge.

Use the diagram below to help you design and build your own cable-stayed bridge. Use straws for the tower, string for the cables, and thin cardboard for the deck. Fix the tower in a block made of clay.

How can you make sure the weight is evenly balanced? What happens if it is not?

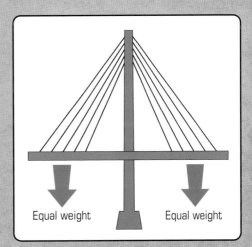

Equal weight   Equal weight

All the parts of the Langkawi Sky Bridge were made on the ground then transported by helicopter up the mountain. Each piece of the deck was going to be lowered into place by helicopter. This worked for the first section, but the helicopter pilot had a problem with the second section. He could not keep the piece steady enough for workers below to attach it.

Engineers had to quickly come up with a solution. They decided to use a cable and **winch** system. Winches were built on platforms at either end of the bridge. The winch cable was then connected to the tower. Each piece of the deck was lifted into place by the winch.

The deck is only 6 feet (1.8 m) wide. When completed, the bridge linked two mountains 410 feet (125 m) apart.

winch—a lifting device in which a cable winds around a revolving drum

In 2012 some changes were made to the Langkawi Sky Bridge. More steel was added to the whole structure to make it even stronger. Also, part of the walkway was replaced with glass so people could look down at the mountain beneath their feet.

A form of transport called the SkyGlide was also added. Before, a cable car carried people up the mountain. But then they had to walk along a trail on the mountainside to reach the bridge. The SkyGlide runs between the cable car station and the bridge.

A cable car carries visitors from ground level to a station on the mountain.

For centuries people have found ways to build bigger, stronger, and more beautiful bridges. The unusual Sky Bridge proves how far bridge design has come. But architects and engineers will continue to imagine and build amazing structures. Who knows where the bridges of the future might lead?

Did You Know?

The Langkawi Sky Bridge has an unusual curved shape. This is so that people can look at the scenery from different angles. Wyss also chose this shape because he did not want visitors to be able to see the end of the bridge from its start. He felt this would encourage people to look at the beauty around them instead of straight ahead.

GLOSSARY

abutment (uh-BUT-muhnt)—a concrete support at the end of a bridge

aqueduct (AK-wuh-duhkt)—an artificial channel for carrying water, typically a large bridge across a river or valley

assembly line (uh-SEM-blee LYN)—an arrangement where work passes from one person to the next person until the job is done

battlement (BA-tuhl-muhnt)—a low wall (as at the top of a castle or a tower) with open spaces to shoot through

bearing (BAYR-ing)—the part of a bridge that the main deck or walkway rests on at each end

channel (CHA-nuhl)—a path that directs water through or across something

engineer (en-juh-NEER)—someone trained to design and build machines, vehicles, bridges, roads, or other structures

foundation (foun-DAY-shuhn)—a base on which something rests or is built

gorge (GORJ)—a canyon with steep walls that rise straight upward

granite (GRAN-it)—a very hard rock used in construction

historian (hi-STAWR-ee-uhn)—a person who studies events that happened in the past

lime (LYM)—a white substance that is made by burning limestone and used to make cement

limestone (LYM-stohn)—a hard rock formed from the remains of ancient sea creatures

parallel (PA-ruh-lel)—an equal distance apart at all points

pier (peer)—an upright structure that supports a bridge or arch

piling (PYL-ing)—a heavy wood or steel pole or beam that is driven into the ground to support a bridge or pier

quarry (KWOR-ee)—a place where stone or other minerals are dug from the ground

rivet (RIV-it)—a metal bolt or pin used to hold together pieces of metal

scaffolding (SKAF-uhl-ding)—a temporary framework or set of platforms used to support workers and materials

span (SPAN)—the length of a bridge from end to end

spring (SPREENG)—a place where water rises to the surface from an underground source

steel (STEEL)—a hard, strong metal made from mostly iron and carbon

strait (STRAYT)—a narrow waterway connecting two large bodies of water

truss (TRUHSS)—a framework of metal or wooden beams used to support objects, such as bridges, walls, or roofs

winch (WIN-tch)—a lifting device in which a cable winds around a revolving drum

READ MORE

Aloian, Sam. *How a Bridge Is Built*. Engineering in Our World. New York: Gareth Stevens, 2016.

Loh-Hagan, Virginia. *Bridges*. Extraordinary Engineering. Ann Arbor, Mich.: Cherry Lake Publishing, 2017.

Spray, Sally. *Bridges*. Awesome Engineering. North Mankato, Minn.: Capstone Press, 2018.

INTERNET SITES

Use FactHound to find Internet sites related to this book.

Visit www.facthound.com

Just type in 9781543529074 and go.

CRITICAL THINKING QUESTIONS

1. Describe the different ways that concrete is used in bridge-building. Use details from the text to support your answers.

2. Imagine you were in the crowd on the day in 1930 when the two halves of the Sydney Harbour Bridge were joined. Write a diary entry describing what you saw and how you felt about it.

3. Imagine you have been asked to design a bridge to cross a deep gorge. Decide whether you would create a suspension bridge or a cable-stayed bridge. Bear in mind factors such as wind, the amount of weight it may need to carry, and how you want it to look.

Check out projects, games and lots more at
www.capstonekids.com

INDEX